The Novice Guide to Book Publishing

Dr. Dawn McLucas

PBK ISBN   9798987503058

BluePrint Ambitions
blueprintambitions.com
Indianapolis, IN

MEET DR. DAWN MCLUCAS

In 2022, Dr. Dawn McLucas founded BluePrint Ambitions. BluePrint Ambitions is a two-fold learning hub. The first component is the authorship and publishing of encouraging and educational books. The second component is digital courses on a range of educational topics.

Dr. McLucas has authored books for adults, children's reading books, children's activity books, and has also created journals, planners, and workbooks to assist others in growth and learning. She has a passion for writing and has published books via hybrid and self-publishing methods.

MISSION STATEMENT

BluePrint
Ambitions

The mission of BluePrint Ambitions is to provide educational and encouraging books and courses that motivate and allow children and adults to grow, learn, and reach goals. You can learn more at blueprintambitions.com.

The purpose of this book is to provide new writers and authors with a foundation, tools, and resources that allow them to confidently assess their options and navigate the publishing process.

Contents

Introduction

Congratulations on taking the first steps toward publishing your work! Embarking on this thrilling adventure as an author is a testament to your creativity, dedication, and love for storytelling. The world of publishing is a vast and diverse landscape, offering endless possibilities and opportunities for your literary dreams to come true. As you set forth on this journey, let the excitement and anticipation fuel your determination, and let your passion for writing be your guiding light.

From the traditional world of publishing with established publishing houses to the empowering realm of self-publishing, and the innovative realm of hybrid models, we will delve into the unique opportunities, benefits, and considerations each path presents. Whether you dream of seeing your work on the shelves of renowned bookstores or are eager to take full control of your creative destiny, this book will equip you with valuable insights to guide you in choosing the best path for your writing aspirations. Embrace the knowledge that you hold the power to bring your stories to life, and each path you explore will lead you closer to fulfilling your dreams of becoming a published author. So, let's unlock the secrets of understanding the different paths to publication!

1

TRADTIONAL

Publishing

Chapter 1: Traditional Publishing

Through reputable publishing houses, traditional publishing offers a tried-and-true method to get your work into readers' hands. Even while the procedure might appear difficult, it can be very satisfying. Let's examine the fundamental elements of conventional publishing.

Literary agents serve as a liaison between authors and publishers, promoting your work and pursuing favorable terms for you in contract negotiations. They have contacts and industry experience that can greatly increase your chances of being published. Find agents that have handled works in your genre or area of interest, and make sure they are still taking submissions. To improve your chances of getting their attention, research their submission requirements and make your enquiry unique. Your query letter introduces yourself to the agent and gives a quick overview of the idea, genre, and word count of your book. Include a compelling synopsis of your novel that highlights the main theme, major players, and distinguishing qualities that make your manuscript stand out. In addition, create an author's biography to show your potential as an author, emphasize your writing experience, pertinent accomplishments, and any platforms you have created.

Chapter 1: Traditional Publishing

Each traditional publisher will have different manuscript submission guidelines and timeframes. Comply with accepted industry standards for manuscript formatting. Use a legible font in 12-point size (such Times New Roman or Arial), double-spaced lines, and one-inch margins. Before submitting, make sure your writing has gone through a thorough editing process and is error-free. The appeal of your manuscript to agencies and publishers can be considerably increased with professional editing.

When an author signs a book contract in traditional publishing, they frequently receive an advance against future revenues. This advance fluctuates according to how well the publisher thinks the book will do. Authors receive royalties from book sales, which are normally calculated as a portion of the book's cover price. The format (e.g., hardback, paperback, ebook) and the author's contract affect royalties in different ways. Publishers may also have special requirements or preferences if your book needs illustrations, whether it is a picture book or an illustrated nonfiction piece. While some publishers might supply an illustrator, others might want you to work with one.

Chapter 1: Traditional Publishing

The procedure for traditional publishing can take some time. It can take months or even years to get your book published, starting with the querying of agents and ending with a publication agreement. The actual publication date may be set several months or even a year after you sign a contract, giving plenty of time for editing, cover design, and marketing initiatives. Keep in mind that the road to traditional publishing demands tenacity and an awareness of the dynamics of the sector. Although rejections are a regular part of the process, each one advances your search for the ideal reader for your work. Maintain your persistence and trust in your work's value.

2

HYBRID

Publishing

Chapter 2: Hybrid Publishing

With hybrid publishing, authors have more control over their work while still receiving professional support and distribution. Hybrid publishing offers a special blending of the greatest parts of traditional and self-publishing. In order to produce a top-notch book, authors work with publishing experts while maintaining creative control. In contrast to traditional publishing, hybrid publishers typically accept a greater range of genres and topics, giving authors more chances to have their work published.

Hybrid publishing frequently requires writers to make financial contributions to the publication process, covering costs for things like editing, cover design, and distribution. The reputable hybrid publishers are transparent about costs from the outset. Be cautious of publishers who make unrealistic promises or demand excessive upfront fees.

Hybrid publishers typically provide professional editing and proofreading services to ensure the manuscript meets industry standards. Authors collaborate with designers to create eye-catching covers and professionally formatted book interiors. Authors of picture books or books that require illustrations can work with the hybrid publisher's team to integrate artwork seamlessly into the book.

Chapter 2: Hybrid Publishing

It's essential to clarify the rights and ownership of illustrations, ensuring that both the author and the illustrator are appropriately credited and compensated. Hybrid publishing generally has quicker production timelines compared to traditional publishing. Authors can see their books in print within a few months after finalizing the manuscript. While hybrid publishing offers speed, it's crucial to maintain high-quality standards throughout the production process. Hybrid publishers often provide distribution through online retailers and bookstores, giving authors broader exposure for their books.

Authors play an active role in marketing their books, but hybrid publishers may offer guidance, tools, and support to maximize the book's visibility. Take the time to research and vet potential hybrid publishers. Look for reviews and testimonials from other authors to assess their reputation and track record.

Before committing to a hybrid publishing agreement, review the contract carefully to understand the terms, rights, and responsibilities of both parties. Hybrid publishing offers a middle ground for authors who desire more creative control while benefiting from professional expertise. By understanding the costs, collaboration, and distribution involved, authors can make an informed decision on whether hybrid publishing aligns with their goals and vision for their book.

3

SELF

Publishing

Chapter 3: Self-Publishing

Self-publishing has revolutionized the publishing industry, providing authors with unprecedented control over their creative work and the opportunity to connect directly with their audience. Embrace the empowering choice of self-publishing and embark on your journey with confidence.

As a self-published author, you retain complete creative control over every aspect of your book, from the writing style to the cover design. Self-publishing allows authors to explore niche topics and genres that might not be as commercially viable for traditional publishers.

Self-publishing requires authors to cover the costs of editing, formatting, cover design, and marketing. These expenses can vary depending on the scope of the project and professional services sought. Unlike traditional publishing, where royalties are shared with the publisher, self-published authors earn a higher percentage of book sales. Authors receive direct payments from retailers or distributors.

Investing in professional editing can help to ensure your book meets the highest literary standards. An editor can provide valuable feedback, catch errors, and help polish your work. Properly formatting your manuscript for various publishing platforms ensures a visually appealing and readable final product.

Chapter 3: Self-Publishing

For books that require illustrations, self-published authors can collaborate with illustrators directly to bring their vision to life. Clearly define the rights and ownership of illustrations in a written agreement to avoid future complications. Self-publishing grants authors the freedom to set their publication schedule. Whether you choose a rapid release or a more deliberate timeline, the decision is yours. While self-publishing allows for flexibility, remember that quality writing, editing, and design are essential for a successful book.

Amazon Kindle Direct Publishing (KDP), Apple Books, Google Play Books, and other platforms offer self-publishing services and global distribution. Utilize these print on demand (POD) services to ensure your book is available in paperback format without the need for large print runs or inventory storage. Establish an author platform, including a website, blog, and active social media presence to connect with your readers. Plan a strategic book launch to generate initial buzz and visibility for your book. Utilize email lists, social media advertising, and book promotions to reach your target audience. Self-publishing empowers authors to make their creative vision a reality. Authors can bypass the traditional gatekeepers and reach readers directly. With careful planning, authors can achieve both artistic fulfillment and commercial success on their creative journey.

4

AVOIDING

Scams

Chapter 4: Avoiding Scams

To safeguard yourself and your work against frauds and unethical acts, it is crucial for aspiring authors to be aware of any potential red flags in the publishing industry. It takes caution and awareness to navigate the publishing market because there are dishonest people and businesses attempting to take advantage of aspiring authors. To ensure your safety and the safety of your work, watch out for warning signs.

It can be beneficial to look up the Better Business Bureau rating of any publishing service or company before working with them. Multiple complaints or a poor rating may be a red flag. You should also be skeptical of any publisher or service provider that promises instant success, bestseller status, or guaranteed sales. Publishing success depends on numerous factors, including quality, market demand, and effective marketing efforts. Scammers may make exaggerated claims about their services, such as offering "exclusive" marketing opportunities at exorbitant prices. Research and compare prices and services offered by multiple providers to ensure they align with industry standards.

Remember, thorough research, cautious decision-making, and seeking advice from professionals when needed, can protect you from publishing scams. Trust your instincts, ask questions, and only engage with individuals or companies who demonstrate professionalism, transparency, and a genuine commitment to helping authors succeed.

Chapter 4: Avoiding Scams

I encourage you to be cautious of overly positive reviews that seem too good to be true. Genuine reviews are often a mix of positive and constructive feedback. I also recommend looking for reviews and testimonials on third-party websites or author forums to get unbiased opinions.

It is also important to vet potential illustrators, artists, editors, and publishers. If you're working with an illustrator, ensure they have a professional portfolio showcasing their work and style. It is a good idea to also clarify the rights and ownership of illustrations in a written agreement to avoid potential disputes later. It is crucial to verify the legitimacy and reputation of a publishing house before submitting your manuscript or signing a contract. You should be cautious of publishers who ask for large upfront fees or offer unrealistic promises of success without credible evidence. Furthermore, a legitimate publisher or service provider will have a professional-looking website with clear information about their offerings and contact details. You should look for transparent pricing, services offered, and terms of agreement on their website. Be wary of companies that withhold critical information or use vague language. Vanity publishers require authors to pay substantial fees to publish their books, often without providing professional editing, distribution and other services.

Chapter 4: Avoiding Scams

Protecting your work and financial interests is vital as an author in the publishing industry. Copyright protection grants you exclusive rights to your creative work, including books, manuscripts, and illustrations. It prevents others from reproducing, distributing, or profiting from your work without permission. While copyright automatically applies to your original work upon creation, registering your copyright with the relevant government agency (e.g., the U.S. Copyright Office) provides additional legal benefits in case of infringement.

It is also important to review publishing contracts in depth. Before signing any contracts with publishers, agents, or service providers, review the terms thoroughly. Seek legal advice if needed to ensure your rights are protected and there are no unfavorable clauses. If hiring illustrators or ghostwriters, ensure you have written agreements that clearly establish your ownership of the resulting work.

Finances is an area where you want to make sure you are using your funds wisely and efficiently. Self-publishing and certain hybrid publishing models require upfront financial investment. Create a budget that covers editing, design, marketing, and other publishing expenses to avoid financial strain. Maintain detailed records of all financial transactions related to your publishing journey. This includes expenses, royalties, and any tax-related documents.

Chapter 4: Avoiding Scams

When working with publishers, agents, or service providers, choose secure payment methods to protect your financial information. Clearly understand the royalty structure and payment schedule outlined in your contracts. Ensure you receive regular and transparent updates on book sales and earnings.

If sharing excerpts or illustrations online, consider adding watermarks or copyright notices to deter unauthorized use. Protect your digital manuscripts, illustrations, and marketing materials with secure passwords and file encryption. Be cautious of unsolicited offers for publishing, marketing, or editing services. Thoroughly research any company or individual before committing to their services.
Verify the legitimacy and reputation of potential service providers through online reviews, testimonials, and industry forums. Consider joining author organizations and writer communities. These groups can offer support, advice, and warnings about potential scams or unscrupulous players in the industry.

By proactively protecting your work and financial interests, you can focus on your writing and publishing journey with greater peace of mind. Stay informed, be diligent, and seek professional assistance when needed to ensure your creative efforts are respected and rewarded as they deserve to be.

5

GHOST

Writers

Chapter 5: Ghostwriters

Ghostwriting is a collaborative writing process where a professional writer, known as a ghostwriter, is hired to create content on behalf of another person, the author, who will take credit for the work. Ghostwriting is prevalent across various literary forms, including books, articles, blog posts, speeches, and even social media content. Let's explore the concept of ghostwriting and its potential benefits for authors.

Not every author possesses the time, writing expertise, or specific knowledge required to craft a compelling and polished manuscript. Ghostwriters bring their writing skills and experience to complement the author's vision. Writing a book is a time-consuming endeavor. Ghostwriting allows authors to focus on other aspects of their lives or careers while entrusting the writing process to a professional. A skilled ghostwriter can capture the author's unique voice, style, and tone, ensuring the final work feels authentic and aligns with the author's personality or brand.

Authors often have brilliant ideas but struggle to articulate them effectively. A ghostwriter can transform these ideas into a well-structured and engaging narrative. Ghostwriters may possess expertise in niche subjects, making them ideal for tackling complex or technical topics that require in-depth knowledge. Ghostwriters can distill complex information into reader-friendly content, making it accessible to a broader audience.

Chapter 5: Ghostwriters

Some individuals, such as celebrities or public figures, may want to share their stories or ideas without revealing their identities. Ghostwriting allows authors to maintain anonymity while sharing their experiences. In the corporate world, executives or entrepreneurs might use ghostwriters to create articles, books, or leadership pieces without dedicating personal time to writing.

Ghostwriters are professionals accustomed to meeting deadlines. Hiring a ghostwriter can expedite the writing process, ensuring the book is completed in a timely manner. Ghostwriters may be able to dedicate focused time to the project, resulting in a faster turnaround compared to the author writing alone.

Successful ghostwriting projects involve open communication between the author and the ghostwriter. This collaboration ensures that the author's vision is at the core of the work. Ghostwriters often provide valuable feedback to improve the manuscript, elevating the overall quality of the book. It's essential for authors to find a reputable and trustworthy ghostwriter who shares their vision and values. A well-executed ghostwriting partnership can result in a beautifully written book that resonates with readers and fulfills the author's objectives, ultimately enhancing their reputation and influence in their respective field.

Chapter 5: Ghostwriters

Choosing the right ghostwriter is a critical step in ensuring a successful and harmonious collaboration that elevates your voice and brings your ideas to life.

Before seeking a ghostwriter, clearly outline your project's scope, goals, and the specific outcomes you hope to achieve. Determine the tone, style, and target audience for your book or content. Ghostwriting services vary widely in cost. Decide on a budget range that aligns with your project's complexity and your expectations for quality.

Look for ghostwriters who have experience and expertise in your genre or subject matter. A ghostwriter with relevant knowledge can bring depth and authenticity to your work. Request writing samples or a portfolio of previous works to assess the ghostwriter's style and versatility. Look for consistency in writing quality across different projects. Ask fellow authors, literary agents, or publishing professionals for recommendations. Personal referrals often lead to successful partnerships. Read testimonials or reviews from previous clients to gain insights into the ghostwriter's professionalism, communication skills, and ability to meet deadlines.

Chapter 5: Ghostwriters

Schedule an initial consultation with potential ghostwriters. Assess their communication style, responsiveness, and willingness to listen to your ideas. A successful ghostwriting partnership requires trust and a strong rapport. Ensure you feel comfortable collaborating with the ghostwriter and that they understand your vision.

Clearly outline the scope of work, deliverables, and expectations. Discuss the level of involvement you desire in the writing process. Agree on a realistic timeline for completing the project. A well-planned schedule ensures that both you and the ghostwriter can meet deadlines effectively. Formalize the terms of your collaboration in a written contract. Include project milestones, payment schedule, confidentiality clauses, and copyright ownership. Decide upfront whether you want your name to appear as the author or if you prefer to retain full ownership and credit for the work.

Finding the perfect ghostwriter is a crucial investment in producing a high-quality and impactful piece of writing. By conducting thorough research, communicating effectively, and defining clear expectations, you can form a productive partnership that elevates your voice and turns your ideas into a compelling narrative that resonates with your readers.

6

PEN

Names

Chapter 6: Pen Names

A pen name, usually referred to as a pseudonym, has been used by writers for decades. It involves creating content and publishing it under a pen name other than their own. Individuals use pen names for various reasons.

Writers, particularly those who write in delicate or contentious genres, may want to protect their privacy and avoid having their real identities revealed to the general public. Differentiating by genre allows certain authors to write for a variety of readers. For each genre, using a separate pen name helps readers understand what to expect from each book. Some writers of nonfiction utilize pen names. In non-fiction, some authors use pen names to establish authority in a specific field, especially when writing about personal experiences or self-help topics. In addition, some historical biases or reader expectations may lead authors to use gender-neutral pen names to avoid potential discrimination or pigeonholing based on their gender. In some cases, publishers may also suggest pen names to fit a particular brand or marketing strategy.

Choosing a pen name can be an interesting process. There are infinite options. The pen name decision may happen quickly or it may take a significant amount of time. Choose a name that resonates with your genre, target audience, or the overall tone of your writing. Ensure the pen name is unique and not already associated or trademarked with another author to avoid confusion or legal issues.

Chapter 6: Pen Names

Social media can be used for creation of pen name branding. Create consistent branding by using the pen name on your author website, social media accounts, and other online platforms. You may also want to set up an email address using the pen name to communicate with publishers, agents, and readers. If you have a literary agent or are working with a publisher, communicate your intention to use a pen name early in the process. Ensure that your pen name is clearly stated in your publishing contracts and that the copyright of your work reflects the pen name.

Once you've established your pen name, introduce yourself to readers using this name through author interviews, book signings, and other public appearances. Be sure to engage with your readers under the pen name on social media and your author website to create a consistent and recognizable presence. If you write in multiple genres under different pen names, carefully manage each persona's online presence and brand to avoid confusion. Using a pen name can be a strategic decision that allows authors to protect their privacy, explore different genres, or create distinct author identities. With thoughtful consideration and effective branding, authors can successfully adopt a pen name and connect with their readers authentically.

Chapter 6: Pen Names

Once you've chosen a pen name and decided to publish your work under this persona, it's essential to build a strong brand behind your pseudonym. A well-crafted brand helps establish your author identity, connects with your target audience, and fosters a lasting relationship with readers. Determine the genre or genres in which you write and the themes that resonate with your work. This will shape the foundation of your brand. Develop a clear vision of the author persona you want to portray. Consider how you want readers to perceive you, your writing style, and your overall image.

Your website should prominently feature your books, covers, and any accolades or awards you've received. Craft an engaging author biography that provides insights into your writing journey and your passion for storytelling. Maintain a blog or news section where you can share updates, writing tips, and engage with your readers. Identify the social media platforms that align with your target audience and genre. Common platforms include Twitter, Facebook, Instagram, and Goodreads. Interact regularly with your followers, respond to comments, and participate in discussions related to your books or genre.

Consider creating a unique author logo or symbol that represents your pen name and is consistent across your online presence and promotional materials. Establish a consistent color scheme and design aesthetic that reflects the tone and themes of your writing.

Chapter 6: Pen Names

Invest in a professional book cover design that reflects the genre and style of your writing. Memorable book covers can make a significant impact on potential readers. Write guest blog posts on relevant websites or participate in interviews to introduce yourself and your work to new audiences. Seek opportunities to be a guest on podcasts or participate in book clubs to increase your visibility and connect with readers.

Develop a catchy and memorable tagline that captures the essence of your author brand and writing. Ensure that your communication across all platforms reflects your author persona's voice and tone. Participate in author communities, forums, or writing groups where you can share experiences and learn from other writers. Attend book signings, literary events, and festivals to network with readers and other authors in your genre.

Building a brand behind your pseudonym is a gradual process that requires consistency and dedication. As you grow your online presence, engage with readers, and produce compelling works, your pen name will become synonymous with quality storytelling and a strong author identity, fostering a loyal and supportive readership.

7

THE
Marketing

Chapter 7: The Marketing

Crafting an effective book marketing strategy involves various essential elements, and one critical aspect is determining the right price for your book. Setting the appropriate price requires careful consideration to strike a balance between attracting readers and ensuring your work is valued appropriately.

It is important to know your target market. Understand your target audience's preferences, spending habits, and the price range they are willing to pay for books in your genre. Consider conducting market research or seeking feedback from beta readers to gain valuable insights. Factor in the expenses associated with producing your book, including editing, cover design, formatting, and printing (if applicable). The price should cover these costs while still allowing you to earn a reasonable profit. Research books in your genre that are similar in length, style, and content. Analyze their pricing strategies to gain an understanding of market trends and where your book fits within the competitive landscape. While it's essential to value your work appropriately, consider offering competitive pricing, especially if you're a new or emerging author. Lower introductory prices or limited-time discounts can attract readers and create momentum for your book.

Chapter 7: The Marketing

If you're publishing both ebook and print editions, consider setting slightly lower prices for ebooks to appeal to budget-conscious readers. Print books typically have higher production costs, so set prices accordingly.

KDP Select and Kindle Countdown Deals

If you're enrolled in Amazon's KDP Select program, you can take advantage of promotional features like Kindle Countdown Deals to offer time-limited discounts. Such promotions can boost visibility and attract readers.

Special Promotions and Pre-Order Discounts

Offer special promotions, discounted pre-orders, or bundle deals to incentivize readers to purchase your book during launch periods or special occasions. Limited-time offers can create a sense of urgency and drive sales.

Monitor Sales and Adjust

Keep a close eye on your book's sales performance and adjust the price as needed. If you notice a decline in sales, consider experimenting with different price points to find the optimal balance.

Leverage Free Promotions (for Ebooks)

For ebooks, consider occasional free promotions, especially for the first book in a series or as part of a marketing campaign. Free promotions can attract new readers, generate reviews, and potentially lead to increased sales for other books in the series.

Chapter 7: The Marketing

While competitive pricing is essential, don't undervalue your work. Remember the effort, time, and creativity invested in your writing. Price your book in a way that reflects its quality and the value you believe it brings to readers.

Setting book prices is an integral part of your book marketing strategy. As you navigate this aspect of publishing, be open to experimentation and adaptation. Strive to find the sweet spot where your book is priced competitively, and its worth is acknowledged by your readers. Remember that successful book marketing involves a multifaceted approach, and the right pricing strategy is a key element in reaching your target audience and achieving your publishing goals.

An author platform is an essential tool for connecting with your readers, building your online presence, and promoting your books effectively. It enables you to showcase your writing, engage with your audience, and establish yourself as a reputable author within your genre. A well-executed book launch and strategic promotions are essential for reaching your target audience, generating buzz around your book, and maximizing its potential success.

Chapter 7: The Marketing

Pre-release marketing is a good way to build anticipation for your book release. Start promoting your book well in advance of the launch date. Create teasers, cover reveals, and sneak peeks to pique readers' interest and build anticipation. Utilize your email list to notify subscribers about the upcoming release and offer pre-order incentives, such as exclusive content or limited-time discounts.

Virtual launch parties can also help boost your book visibility. Organize a virtual book launch event where you can read excerpts, interact with readers, and answer questions. Utilize platforms like Zoom or Facebook Live for broader reach. Coordinate book signings at local bookstores or venues, inviting friends, family, and fans to attend and create word-of-mouth buzz.

Collaborative promotions are a valuable method to reach potential readers. Partner with other authors in your genre for joint promotions, bundle deals, or collaborative giveaways. This exposes your book to their readers and vice versa. Seek endorsements or reviews from influencers, bloggers, and book reviewers within your genre. Positive reviews can significantly impact your book's visibility and credibility.

Chapter 7: The Marketing

Social media marketing is vital to marketing. Create engaging social media posts with visuals, quotes from your book, and behind-the-scenes insights. Encourage discussions and interactions with your audience. Produce a captivating book trailer to share on social media and YouTube, giving readers a visual glimpse into your story. Social media contests can be used to host giveaways on your social media platforms, encouraging readers to share your book and posts for a chance to win a signed copy or other book-related goodies.

Book discounts and giveaways can help authors attract new customers. Offer your book at a discounted price during the initial launch phase to entice readers to make an immediate purchase. Consider a limited-time free promotion for your ebook to attract a broader readership and encourage reviews and word-of-mouth recommendations. Run a book giveaway on Goodreads to engage with its vast community of avid readers and potential reviewers.

Book reviews can also create more interest in your writing. You may want to consider distributing advance reader copies (ARCs) to book bloggers, influencers, and early reviewers to generate buzz and obtain early reviews before the official launch. In addition, you can also seek professional editorial reviews from reputable sources to boost credibility and visibility.

Chapter 7: The Marketing

Book marketing services are also available tools for increasing the reach of your book. Consider investing in book marketing services or promotions through platforms like BookBub, BookBub Ads, or Amazon Advertising to reach a wider audience and increase book visibility. Remember that effective book launches and promotions require careful planning, a strong online presence, and active engagement with your readers. Be persistent in promoting your book even after the launch, and don't be afraid to experiment with different marketing tactics to find what works best for your audience. With a strategic approach, you can successfully connect with your readers, build a loyal fan base, and propel your book towards success.

.

8

AWARDS AND

Rewards

Chapter 8: Awards and Rewards

Participating in awards and literary competitions can be a significant and rewarding aspect of an author's journey. Winning or even being nominated for prestigious awards can have a profound impact on an author's career and book sales.

Recognition and credibility are potential rewards for authors. Awards and nominations serve as validation of an author's talent and dedication to their craft. It lends credibility to the quality of their writing and the value of their book. Winning or being shortlisted for a notable award elevates an author's reputation within the literary community and among readers.

Award-winning books often gain increased media attention and visibility. This exposure can attract new readers and broaden the book's audience. Winning an award or being a finalist can lead to a surge in book sales as readers are more likely to trust and invest in critically acclaimed works. Awards and recognition can capture the attention of literary agents and publishers, potentially leading to new opportunities for the author. An award-winning book may command more favorable terms in book deals, including advances and marketing support.

Chapter 8: Awards and Rewards

Networking and professional growth is another possible reward for authors. Participation in literary competitions and awards ceremonies allows authors to connect with other writers, agents, and industry professionals, fostering valuable relationships.

The process of preparing submissions and attending events can provide authors with opportunities to refine their presentation skills and learn from peers. The recognition and affirmation that awards provide can serve as a powerful motivator for authors to continue honing their craft and producing new work. Winning or being acknowledged in competitions can instill greater confidence in an author's creative abilities and writing choices.

Differentiation in the market can set apart your books. In a competitive publishing landscape, awards set a book apart from others, helping it to stand out in a saturated market. Award-winning books are more likely to garner media coverage and attention from book reviewers. Furthermore, Literary awards celebrate outstanding literary achievements and contribute to the preservation of literary excellence and diversity. Authors should be selective about the awards and competitions they choose to enter, focusing on those that align with their genre and writing style. While winning awards is undoubtedly a valuable achievement, the process of submitting to competitions can also offer personal and professional growth.

Chapter 8: Awards and Rewards

There are numerous book awards that are available for authors. Submitting your work to awards and competitions requires thoughtful preparation and a strategic approach to maximize your chances of recognition. Here are essential tips to help you effectively submit your work and increase your likelihood of receiving accolades:

1. Identify Appropriate Awards
Research and target awards and competitions that align with your genre, writing style, and the theme of your book. Look for well-established and reputable organizations or literary institutions.

2. Review Submission Guidelines
Carefully read the submission guidelines for each award. Pay attention to eligibility criteria, submission formats, word counts, and deadlines.

3. Prepare a Polished Manuscript
Ensure your manuscript is polished, free of errors, and professionally edited. Submit your best possible work to make a strong impression on judges.

4.Tailor Your Submission
If the competition requires a specific excerpt or sample, select a compelling section that showcases your writing prowess and the essence of your book.

Chapter 8: Awards and Rewards

It is important to prepare a strong submission package for potential awards. Craft a well-written cover letter introducing yourself and your book. Express your appreciation for the opportunity to be considered for the award and highlight any relevant credentials. Include a concise and engaging synopsis of your book, emphasizing its unique elements and the themes it explores. Provide a concise and impactful author biography that showcases your writing experience and achievements. Submit your work well before the deadline to ensure ample time for processing and to avoid technical issues. Adhere strictly to the submission guidelines to avoid disqualification. Submit the required materials in the specified format and ensure all necessary documents are included.

After submitting your work, be patient during the evaluation and judging process. Some awards may take several months to announce the results. Regardless of the outcome, accept the results graciously. Whether you win or not, participating in competitions is an opportunity for growth and exposure. Maintain a record of all the awards and competitions you've submitted to, including submission dates, results, and feedback received. If possible, request feedback from the judges or organizers to gain insights into how to improve your future submissions. By conducting thorough research, presenting your best work, and following submission guidelines diligently, you can maximize your chances of recognition in awards and competitions.

Chapter 8: Awards and Rewards

There are unlimited rewards for authors. The rewards will not be the same for all authors. The publishing journey is filled with milestones and achievements, big and small, that mark significant progress and growth as an author. Celebrating these moments not only boosts morale and motivation but also provides an opportunity to acknowledge the hard work and dedication invested in your writing career.

Whether you win or become a finalist in a competition or award, take pride in this accomplishment. Share the news with your followers and express gratitude to those who supported you. If possible, attend award ceremonies to network with fellow authors and industry professionals, celebrating the collective achievements of the literary community.

Reaching bestseller status on online platforms or in specific genres is an achievement worth celebrating. Share the news with your audience and express appreciation for their support. Acknowledge sales milestones, such as selling a certain number of copies or hitting a particular revenue target. Consider offering promotions or giveaways to celebrate with your readers. Celebrate any media coverage or interviews you receive. Share links or snippets of the features with your followers to expand your reach.

Chapter 8: Awards and Rewards

It is important to reflect and appreciate your writing experiences. Celebrate by taking time for self-reflection on your journey as an author. Recognize your growth, milestones achieved, and the obstacles you've overcome. Express gratitude to your readers, friends, family, beta readers, critique partners, and everyone who supported you throughout your publishing journey. Celebrating milestones and achievements is not only a reward for your hard work but also an opportunity to share your successes with your audience and community. Embrace each step of your publishing journey with enthusiasm and gratitude, knowing that each milestone brings you closer to your goals as an accomplished author.

Reflect on the passion and love you have for storytelling. Reconnect with your initial motivations for becoming an author to reignite your enthusiasm. Staying motivated as an author requires patience, resilience, and a willingness to learn and grow from challenges. Embrace the journey, celebrate your progress, and remember that perseverance and dedication are keys to realizing your writing dreams. By maintaining a positive mindset and a supportive network, you can overcome obstacles and continue to create meaningful stories that resonate with readers.

Conclusion

It is exciting that you are starting your writing career! Remember that your love of storytelling is the inspiration behind your creativity and the cornerstone of your success as you continue down this fascinating path. With the knowledge that every word you write puts you one step closer to realizing your goals, embrace each stage of your writing journey with confidence.

As an author, your voice is what makes you stand out. Take pride in your original viewpoint, experiences, and creativity. Instead of comparing yourself to others, emphasize your unique style and the enchantment you can create with words. Writing is a constantly changing art. Accept the process of development and progress because it's through these challenges that you'll flourish as a writer. Each page you write, each story you create, and each edit you make will propel you forward on your writing journey. Let your imagination soar. Don't be afraid to explore new genres or experiment with storytelling techniques. Embrace your creativity and let it guide you to new horizons. Your willingness to take risks will lead to unique and extraordinary stories.

Conclusion

Rejections are not setbacks; they are stepping stones to success. Remember that even celebrated authors faced rejections before finding their place in the literary world. Learn from feedback, keep honing your craft, and use rejections as opportunities to grow stronger. Celebrate each achievement, no matter how small. Completing a chapter, receiving praise from a reader, or reaching a writing goal are all reasons to celebrate. Acknowledge your progress and let it fuel your passion for the next leg of your journey.

Dream big and believe in yourself. Your writing journey may lead you down unexpected paths, but never lose sight of your dreams. Visualize your success, set ambitious goals, and take steady steps toward making those dreams a reality. Writing is not just about the destination; it's about the joy of the journey. Embrace the moments of inspiration, the joy of creating characters, and the satisfaction of weaving worlds with your words. Let the process be your refuge, a place where you find solace and fulfillment. Surround yourself with fellow writers who uplift and inspire you. Engage in critique groups, writing workshops, and online communities. A supportive network will be there to cheer you on, celebrate your successes, and lift you up during challenging times.

Conclusion

Your stories have the power to touch hearts, inspire minds, and transport readers to new worlds. Never underestimate the impact of your words. The connection you forge with readers is a testament to the magic of storytelling. Have unwavering belief in your talent and potential as a writer. You are capable of greatness, and your passion will carry you through any doubt or uncertainty. Trust in your ability to craft compelling narratives that resonate with others.

Your writing journey is an adventure full of surprises and awe-inspiring moments. Take it on with unrelenting fire and unbounded confidence. Write from the heart, tell the world about your experiences, and remember that the trip is just as essential as the final goal. You are permanently etching your name into the literary landscape with every word you write. Accept the fun, the difficulties, and the enchantment of writing. The greatest of your journey is still to come; it has only begun. Keep writing with confidence and passion, because the world is waiting to hear your voice.

International Standard Book Number (ISBN)

When considering the different paths to publication, understanding the importance of the International Standard Book Number (ISBN) is essential. An ISBN is a unique identifier assigned to each published book, serving as a universal code that distinguishes your work from other publications. It plays a crucial role in the book supply chain, ensuring accurate tracking, distribution, and sales data for your book.

Traditional Publishing

If you're pursuing traditional publishing and have secured a publishing deal with a reputable publishing house, they will likely handle the ISBN allocation for your book. The publisher will register the ISBN under their name or their imprint, tying it to your book's specific edition.

Self-Publishing

For self-published authors, obtaining an ISBN is typically your responsibility. Each format of your book (e.g., print, ebook) and each edition (e.g., hardcover, paperback) requires a unique ISBN. Many online platforms, such as Amazon Kindle Direct Publishing (KDP) and IngramSpark, offer options to purchase ISBNs or provide free ISBNs for use within their distribution networks.

Hybrid Publishing

The ISBN process for hybrid publishing may vary depending on the publisher's policies. Some hybrid publishers may handle the ISBN assignment, while others might require the author to provide their own. Ensure clear communication with the publisher to understand who is responsible for obtaining the ISBN.

The ISBN is crucial for making your book accessible in the global market. Booksellers, libraries, and online retailers use ISBNs to identify and order books, making it easier for readers to find and purchase your work worldwide. If you plan to publish both ebook and print editions of your book, obtain separate ISBNs for each format. Ebook ISBNs are specific to digital versions, while print ISBNs are for physical copies. This distinction allows for accurate tracking and reporting of sales data for both formats. If you release subsequent editions of your book (e.g., revised, updated, special anniversary editions), each edition should have a unique ISBN. This ensures that the specific edition is identified correctly, allowing readers to distinguish between different versions.

Important Terms- ISBN

ISBNs play a crucial role in metadata and book discovery. Book metadata, which includes ISBN, title, author, genre, and other essential information, is used by search engines, booksellers, and libraries to categorize and display your book to potential readers. One creditable place that you can purchase your own ISBN is bowker.com.

As you embark on your publishing journey, understanding the significance of ISBNs will help you navigate the intricacies of the publishing process more effectively. Whether you're working with a traditional publisher, self-publishing, or exploring hybrid options, the ISBN serves as a fundamental tool in making your book accessible to readers worldwide. Take the time to ensure that each format and edition of your book is correctly identified with its unique ISBN, opening doors to broader distribution and enhancing the discoverability of your literary masterpiece.

The Library of Congress Control Number (LCCN) is a unique identifier assigned by the Library of Congress in the United States to catalog and organize books within its vast collection. While not mandatory for all published books, obtaining an LCCN can offer valuable benefits to authors, especially for those pursuing a broader reach and academic recognition. An LCCN can be applied for on the Library of Congress website www loc.gov.

An LCCN ensures that your book is properly cataloged in the Library of Congress's extensive database. This makes it easier for librarians, researchers, and educators to find and access your work for educational purposes and academic research. Having an LCCN enhances your book's credibility and may increase its chances of being included in academic and institutional libraries. It demonstrates that your work has been reviewed and recognized by a national institution known for preserving knowledge and literature. For authors of scholarly works or non-fiction books, an LCCN can be particularly valuable. Many academic institutions and scholars prefer to access books with LCCNs for their research and citations.

For traditionally published authors, the publisher is typically responsible for obtaining the LCCN. They will include the LCCN on the copyright page of your book before printing and distribution. In hybrid publishing, the publisher will also usually obtain the LCCN. While, authors who self-publish can apply for an LCCN directly from the Library of Congress. The process involves submitting an application with details about the book and its author. While obtaining an LCCN is not mandatory for self-published books, it can provide additional visibility and recognition for your work. To apply for an LCCN, authors can use the Library of Congress website or contact the Cataloging in Publication (CIP) program. The CIP program may also be available through some self-publishing platforms, making the application process more straightforward.

Acquiring an LCCN is a valuable consideration, especially for authors seeking academic recognition, broader accessibility, and a sense of accomplishment in preserving their work within a prestigious national institution. While it may not be a mandatory step in the publishing process, having an LCCN can open doors to academic and institutional recognition, fostering a deeper connection between your book and readers within the scholarly community. As you explore the different paths to publication, consider the potential benefits of obtaining an LCCN and how it may contribute to the long-term success of your literary endeavors.

ADDITIONAL RESOURCES

AMAZON KDP-SELF PUBLISHING

kdp.amazon.com

INGRAMSPARK SELF PUBLISHING

www.ingramspark.com

LULU SELF PUBLISHING

www.lulu.com

LITERARY MARKETPLACE

www.literarymarketplace.com

TRADITIONAL PUBLISHER EXAMPLES

Random House, Simon & Schuster, Harper Collins

HYBRID PUBLISHER EXAMPLES

Bibliokid Publishing, First Edition Design Publishing

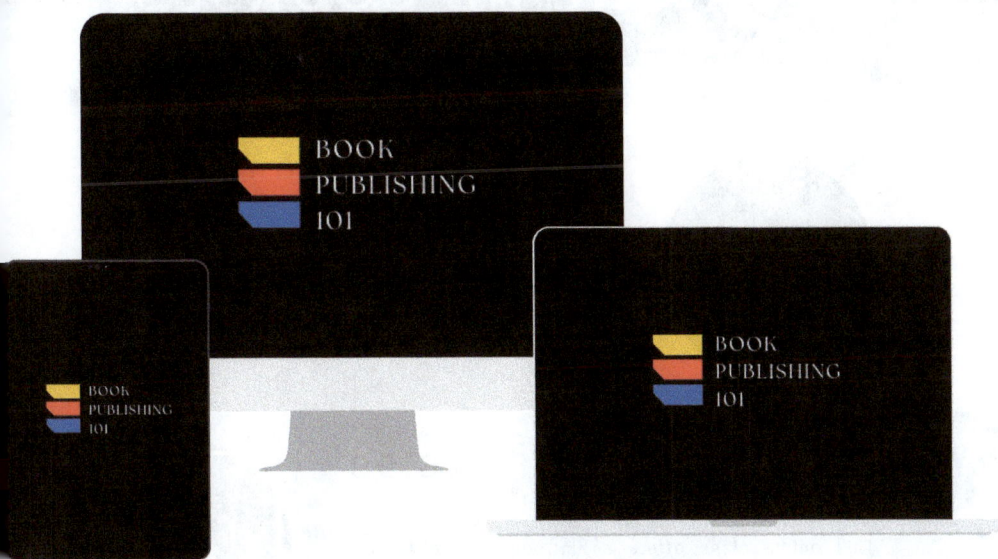

GET THE FULL COURSE!

This book publishing course is the perfect class for new authors. It addresses many of the questions that beginner authors have. The course discusses traditional publishing, hybrid publishing, and self-publishing. The discussion includes areas of cover designs, illustrations, marketing, and more. Let's get you closer to publishing your book.It also offers communication with the course instructor and a private course Facebook Group.

OUR ONLINE COURSES

BOOK PUBLISHING 101

$49

FROM ASPIRING WRITER TO PUBLISHED

This online self-paced, lifetime access course offers new writers and authors information and resources regarding self-publishing, traditional publishing, and hybrid publishing options.

HOW TO DESIGN YOUR OWN BOOK COVER IN CANVA

$6.99

This online class offers an introduction to Canva Software uses and templates. It also includes video demonstrations showing how an eBook cover and a paperback cover can be created in Canva.

HOW TO CREATE A BOOK TRAILER IN CANVA

FREE

This FREE online class discusses Canva software and includes video demonstration on how to create a video book trailer for your book.

blueprintambitions.com

OUR BOOKS

THE NOVICE GUIDE TO BOOK PUBLISHING

$9.99

This guide provides information, tools, and resources to new authors and writers who are looking to learn more about the publishing process, practices, and options. The book covers self-publishing, traditional publishing, and hybrid publishing.

THE NOVEL WORKBOOK: A COMPLETE PLANNER FOR WRITERS AND AUTHORS

$6.99

This 100-page planner includes sections related to the topic, setting, plot, and character development. It also includes lined pages for you to write about anything you want.

CANVA BOOK TEMPLATE

$25

This customizable 150-page book template offers cover examples and multiple organized section options. This template is your one-stop-shop for creating a stunning eBook, paperback, or even a distinguished hardback edition on the topic of your choice.

"

CHOOSE
ADVENTURE.
WRITE YOUR OWN
STORY.

- Dr. Dawn McLucas

"

YES TO
NEW
ADVENTURES

NOTES

NOTES

THE NOVICE GUIDE TO BOOK PUBLISHING

DR. DAWN MCLUCAS

Keep in Touch

✉ BLUEPRINTAMBITIONSLLC
@GMAIL.COM

🌐 WWW.BLUEPRINTAMBITIONS.COM

📷 @BLUEPRINT_AMBITIONS

f WWW.FACEBOOK.COM/DOCDNM